The Key Facts™

on

South Korea

Essential Information on South Korea

By Patrick W. Nee

The Internationalist®

www.internationalist.com

The Internationalist®

International Business, Investment, and Travel

Published by:

The Internationalist Publishing Company

96 Walter Street/ Suite 200

Boston, MA 02131, USA

Tel: 617-354-7722

www.internationalist.com

PN@internationalist.com

Table Of Contents

Chapter 1: Background

An independent kingdom for much of its long history, Korea was occupied by Japan beginning in 1905 following the Russo-Japanese War. In 1910, Tokyo formally annexed the entire Peninsula. Korea regained its independence following Japan's surrender to the United States in 1945. After World War II, a democratic-based government (Republic of Korea, ROK) was set up in the southern half of the Korean Peninsula while a Communist-style government was installed in the north (Democratic People's Republic of Korea, DPRK). During the Korean War (1950-53), U.S. troops and UN forces fought alongside ROK soldiers to defend South Korea from a DPRK invasion supported by China and the Soviet Union. A 1953 armistice split the peninsula along a demilitarized zone at about the 38th parallel. PARK Chung-hee took over leadership of the country in a 1961 coup. During his regime, from 1961 to 1979, South Korea achieved rapid economic growth, with per capita income rising to roughly 17 times the level of North Korea. South Korea held its first free presidential election under a revised democratic constitution in 1987, with former ROK Army general ROH Tae-woo winning a close race. In 1993, KIM Young-sam (1993-98) became South Korea's first civilian president. South Korea today is a fully functioning modern democracy. LEE Myung-bak (2008-2013) pursued a policy of global engagement , highlighted by Seoul's hosting of the G-20 summit in November 2010 and the Nuclear Security Summit in March 2012. South Korea also secured a non-permanent seat (2013-14) on the UN Security Council and will host the 2018 Winter Olympic Games. President PARK Geun-hye took office in February 2013 and is South Korea's first female leader. Serious tensions with North Korea have punctuated inter-Korean relations in recent years, including the North's sinking of the South Korean warship Cheonan in March 2010 and its artillery attack on South Korean soldiers and citizens in November 2010.

Chapter 2: Geography

Location:

> Eastern Asia, southern half of the Korean Peninsula bordering the Sea of Japan and the Yellow Sea

Geographic coordinates:

> 37 00 N, 127 30 E

Map references:

> Asia

Area:

> total: 99,720 sq km
>
> country comparison to the world: 109
>
> land: 96,920 sq km
>
> water: 2,800 sq km

Area - comparative:

> slightly larger than Indiana

Land boundaries:

> total: 238 km
>
> border countries: North Korea 238 km

Coastline:

> 2,413 km

Maritime claims:

> territorial sea: 12 nm; between 3 nm and 12 nm in the Korea Strait
>
> contiguous zone: 24 nm
>
> exclusive economic zone: 200 nm

continental shelf: not specified

Climate:

temperate, with rainfall heavier in summer than winter

Terrain:

mostly hills and mountains; wide coastal plains in west and south

Elevation extremes:

lowest point: Sea of Japan 0 m

highest point: Halla-san 1,950 m

Natural resources:

coal, tungsten, graphite, molybdenum, lead, hydropower potential

Land use:

arable land: 16.58%

permanent crops: 2.01%

other: 81.41% (2005)

Irrigated land:

8,320 sq km (2003)

Total renewable water resources:

69.7 cu km (1999)

Freshwater withdrawal (domestic/industrial/agricultural):

total: 18.59 cu km/yr (36%/16%/48%)

per capita: 389 cu m/yr (2000)

Natural hazards:

occasional typhoons bring high winds and floods; low-level seismic activity common in southwest volcanism: Halla (elev. 1,950 m) is considered historically active although it has not erupted in many centuries

Environment - current issues:

air pollution in large cities; acid rain; water pollution from the discharge of sewage and industrial effluents; drift net fishing

Environment - international agreements:

party to: Antarctic-Environmental Protocol, Antarctic-Marine Living Resources, Antarctic Treaty, Biodiversity, Climate Change, Climate Change-Kyoto Protocol, Desertification, Endangered Species, Environmental Modification, Hazardous Wastes, Law of the Sea, Marine Dumping, Ozone Layer Protection, Ship Pollution, Tropical Timber 83, Tropical Timber 94, Wetlands, Whaling

signed, but not ratified: none of the selected agreements

Geography - note:

strategic location on Korea Strait

Chapter 3: People and Society

Nationality:

noun: Korean(s)

adjective: Korean

Ethnic groups:

homogeneous (except for about 20,000 Chinese)

Languages:

Korean, English (widely taught in junior high and high school)

Religions:

Christian 31.6% (Protestant 24%, Roman Catholic 7.6%), Buddhist 24.2%, other or unknown 0.9%, none 43.3% (2010 survey)

Population:

48,955,203 (July 2013 est.)

country comparison to the world: 25

Age structure:

0-14 years: 14.6% (male 3,717,701/female 3,424,490)

15-24 years: 13.6% (male 3,525,050/female 3,117,198)

25-54 years: 47.8% (male 11,925,181/female 11,491,841)

55-64 years: 11.7% (male 2,842,996/female 2,907,730)

65 years and over: 12.3% (male 2,469,093/female 3,533,923) (2012 est.)

Median age:

total: 39 years

male: 37.6 years

female: 40.4 years (2012 est.)

Population growth rate:

0.204% (2012 est.)

country comparison to the world: 176

Birth rate:

8.42 births/1,000 population (2012 est.)

country comparison to the world: 216

Death rate:

6.38 deaths/1,000 population (July 2012 est.)

country comparison to the world: 153

Net migration rate:

0 migrant(s)/1,000 population (2012 est.)

country comparison to the world: 91

Urbanization:

urban population: 83% of total population (2010)

rate of urbanization: 0.6% annual rate of change (2010-15 est.)

Major cities - population:

SEOUL (capital) 9.778 million; Busan (Pusan) 3.439 million; Incheon (Inch'on) 2.572 million; Daegu (Taegu) 2.458 million; Daejon (Taejon) 1.497 million (2009)

Sex ratio:

at birth: 1.07 male(s)/female

under 15 years: 1.09 male(s)/female

15-64 years: 1.04 male(s)/female

65 years and over: 0.69 male(s)/female

total population: 1 male(s)/female (2011 est.)

Maternal mortality rate:

16 deaths/100,000 live births (2010)

country comparison to the world: 143

Infant mortality rate:

total: 4.08 deaths/1,000 live births

country comparison to the world: 198

male: 4.29 deaths/1,000 live births

female: 3.86 deaths/1,000 live births (2012 est.)

Life expectancy at birth:

total population: 79.3 years

country comparison to the world: 41

male: 76.12 years

female: 82.7 years (2012 est.)

Total fertility rate:

1.24 children born/woman (2013 est.)

country comparison to the world: 219

Health expenditures:

6.9% of GDP (2010)

country comparison to the world: 85

Physicians density:

1.967 physicians/1,000 population (2008)

Hospital bed density:

10.3 beds/1,000 population (2009)

Sanitation facility access:

improved:

>*urban*: 100% of population
>
>*rural*: 100% of population
>
>*total*: 100% of population (2010 est.)

HIV/AIDS - adult prevalence rate:

less than 0.1% (2009 est.)

country comparison to the world: 134

HIV/AIDS - people living with HIV/AIDS:

9,500 (2009 est.)

country comparison to the world: 100

HIV/AIDS - deaths:

fewer than 500 (2009 est.)

country comparison to the world: 90

Obesity - adult prevalence rate:

3.2% (2001)

country comparison to the world: 64

Education expenditures:

5.1% of GDP (2009)

country comparison to the world: 74

Literacy:

definition: age 15 and over can read and write

total population: 97.9%

male: 99.2%

female: 96.6% (2002)

School life expectancy (primary to tertiary education):

total: 17 years

male: 18 years

female: 16 years (2008)

Unemployment, youth ages 15-24:

total: 9.8%

country comparison to the world: 107

male: 11.2%

female: 9% (2010)

Chapter 4: Government and Key Leaders

Country name:

> conventional long form: Republic of Korea
>
> conventional short form: South Korea
>
> local long form: Taehan-min'guk
>
> local short form: Han'guk
>
> abbreviation: ROK

Government type:

> republic

Capital:

> name: Seoul
>
> geographic coordinates: 37 33 N, 126 59 E
>
> time difference: UTC+9 (14 hours ahead of Washington, DC during Standard Time)

Administrative divisions:

> 9 provinces (do, singular and plural), 6 metropolitan cities (gwangyoksi, singular and plural), 1 special city, and 1 special self-governing city
>
> provinces: Chungbuk (North Chungcheong), Chungnam (South Chungcheong), Gangwon, Gyeonggi, Gyeongbuk (North Gyeongsang), Gyeongnam (South Gyeongsang), Jeju, Jeonbuk (North Jeolla), Jeonnam (South Jeolla)
>
> metropolitan cities: Busan (Pusan), Daegu (Taegu), Daejon (Taejon), Gwangju (Kwangju), Incheon (Inch'on), Ulsan

special city: Seoul

special self-governing city: Sejong

Independence:

15 August 1945 (from Japan)

National holiday:

Liberation Day, 15 August (1945)

Constitution:

17 July 1948; note - amended or rewritten many times; current constitution approved 29 October 1987

Legal system:

mixed legal system combining European civil law, Anglo-American law, and Chinese classical thought

International law organization participation:

has not submitted an ICJ jurisdiction declaration; accepts ICCt jurisdiction

Suffrage:

19 years of age; universal

Executive branch:

chief of state: President PARK Geun-hye (since 25 February 2013)

head of government: Prime Minister CHUNG Hong-won (since 26 February 2013)

cabinet: State Council appointed by the president on the prime minister's recommendation

elections: president elected by popular vote for a single five-year term; PARK Geun-hye elected on 19 December

2012; next election to be held in December 2017; prime minister appointed by president with consent of National Assembly

election results: PARK Geun-Hye elected president on 19 December 2012; percent of vote - PARK Geun-Hye (NFP) 51.6%, MOON Jae-In (DUP) 48%, others 0.4%

Legislative branch:

unicameral National Assembly or Gukhoe (300 seats; 246 members elected in single-seat constituencies, 54 elected by proportional representation; members serve four-year terms)

elections: last held on 11 April 2012 (next to be held in April 2016)

election results: percent of vote by party - NA; seats by party - NFP 152, DUP 127, UPP 13, LFP 5, independents 3

Judicial branch:

Supreme Court (justices appointed by the president with consent of National Assembly); Constitutional Court (justices appointed by the president based partly on nominations by National Assembly and Chief Justice of the court)

Political parties and leaders:

Democratic United Party or DUP (formerly the Democratic Party or DP) [MOON Hee-sang (interim)]; Liberty Forward Party or LFP (now part of the NFP); New

Frontier Party (NFP) or Saenuri (formerly Grand National Party) [HWANG Woo-yea]; Progressive Justice Party or PJP [ROH Hoe-chan and CHO Joon-ho]; United Progressive Party or UPP [LEE Jung-hee]

Political pressure groups and leaders:

Catholic Priests' Association for Justice; Citizen's Coalition for Economic Justice; Federation of Korean Industries; Federation of Korean Trade Unions; Korean Confederation of Trade Unions; Korean Veterans' Association; Lawyers for a Democratic Society; National Council of Churches; People's Solidarity for Participatory Democracy

International organization participation:

ADB, AfDB (nonregional member), APEC, ARF, ASEAN (dialogue partner), Australia Group, BIS, CD, CICA, CP, EAS, EBRD, FAO, FATF, G-20, IADB, IAEA, IBRD, ICAO, ICC (national committees), ICRM, IDA, IEA, IFAD, IFC, IFRCS, IHO, ILO, IMF, IMO, IMSO, Interpol, IOC, IOM, IPU, ISO, ITSO, ITU, ITUC (NGOs), LAIA (observer), MIGA, MINURSO, NEA, NSG, OAS (observer), OECD, OPCW, OSCE (partner), Paris Club (associate), PCA, PIF (partner), SAARC (observer), SICA (observer), UN, UNAMID, UNCTAD, UNESCO, UNHCR, UNIDO, UNIFIL, UNISFA, UNMIL, UNMISS, UNMOGIP, UNOCI, UNWTO, UPU, WCO, WHO, WIPO, WMO, WTO, ZC

Diplomatic representation in the US:

chief of mission: Ambassador CHOI Young-jin

chancery: 2450 Massachusetts Avenue NW, Washington, DC 20008

telephone: [1] (202) 939-5600

FAX: [1] (202) 797-0595

consulate(s) general: Agana (Guam), Atlanta, Boston, Chicago, Honolulu, Houston, Los Angeles, New York, San Francisco, Seattle

consulate(s) general: Anchorage

Diplomatic representation from the US:

chief of mission: Ambassador Sung Y. KIM

embassy: 188 Sejong-daero, Jongno-gu, Seoul 110-710

mailing address: US Embassy Seoul, Unit 15550, APO AP 96205-5550

telephone: [82] (2) 397-4200

FAX: [82] (2) 725-0152

Key Leaders:

Pres.	**PARK Geun-hye**
Prime Min.	**CHUNG Hong-won**
Min., Prime Min.'s Office	**YIM Jong-yong**
Min. of Culture, Sports, & Tourism	**YOO Jin-ryong**
Min. of Education, Science, & Technology	**SEO Nam-soo**

Min. of Employment & Labor	**PHANG Ha-nam**
Min. of Environment	**YOON Seong-kyu**
Min. for Food, Agriculture, Forestry, & Fisheries	**LEE Dong-phil**
Min. of Foreign Affairs	**YUN Byung-se**
Min. of Gender Equality & Family	**CHO Yoon-sun**
Min. of Health & Welfare	**CHIN Young**
Min. of Justice	**HWANG Kyo-an**
Min. of Knowledge Economy	**YOON Sang-jick**
Min. of Land, Transport, & Maritime Affairs	**SUH Seoung-hwan**
Min. of National Defense	**KIM Kwan-jin**
Min. of Public Admin. & Security	**YOO Jeong-bok**
Min. of Strategy & Finance	**BAHK Jae-wan**
Min. of Unification	**RYOO Kihl-jae**
Chmn., Anticorruption & Civil Rights Commission	**LEE Sung-bo**
Chmn., Board of Audit & Inspection	**YANG Kun**
Chmn., Fair Trade Commission	**KIM Dong-soo**
Chmn., Financial Services	**KIM Seok-dong**

Commission	
Chmn., Korea Communications Commission	**LEE Kye-cheol**
Chmn., Korea Communications Standards Commission	**PARK Man**
Chmn., Presidential Council on National Competitiveness	**SAKONG Il**
Chmn., National Human Rights Commission	**HYUN Byung-chul**
Chief of Staff, Office of the Pres.	**HUH Tae-yeol**
Senior Presidential Sec. for External Strategies, Office of the Pres.	
Senior Presidential Sec. for Foreign Affairs & Security Policy, Office of the Pres.	**JU Chul-ki**
Dir., National Intelligence Service	**WON Sei-hoon**
Governor, Bank of Korea	**KIM Choong-soo**
Ambassador to the US	**CHOI Young-jin**
Permanent Representative to the UN, New York	**KIM Sook**

Flag description:

white with a red (top) and blue yin-yang symbol in the center; there is a different black trigram from the ancient I Ching (Book of Changes) in each corner of the white field; the Korean national flag is called Taegukki; white is a traditional Korean color and represents peace and purity; the blue section represents the negative cosmic forces of the yin, while the red symbolizes the opposite positive forces of the yang; each trigram (kwae) denotes one of the four universal elements, which together express the principle of movement and harmony

National symbol(s):

taegeuk (yin yang symbol)

National anthem:

name: "Aegukga" (Patriotic Song)

lyrics/music: YUN Ch'i-Ho or AN Ch'ang-Ho/AHN Eaktay

note: adopted 1948, well known by 1910; both North Korea and South Korea's anthems share the same name and have a vaguely similar melody but have different lyrics

Chapter 5: Economy

Economy - overview:

South Korea over the past four decades has demonstrated incredible growth and global integration to become a high-tech industrialized economy. In the 1960s, GDP per capita was comparable with levels in the poorer countries of Africa and Asia. In 2004, South Korea joined the trillion dollar club of world economies, and is currently the world's 12th largest economy. Initially, a system of close government and business ties, including directed credit and import restrictions, made this success possible. The government promoted the import of raw materials and technology at the expense of consumer goods, and encouraged savings and investment over consumption. The Asian financial crisis of 1997-98 exposed longstanding weaknesses in South Korea's development model including high debt/equity ratios and massive short-term foreign borrowing. GDP plunged by 6.9% in 1998, and then recovered by 9% in 1999-2000. Korea adopted numerous economic reforms following the crisis, including greater openness to foreign investment and imports. Growth moderated to about 4% annually between 2003 and 2007. Korea's export focused economy was hit hard by the 2008 global economic downturn, but quickly rebounded in subsequent years, reaching 6.3% growth in

2010. The US-South Korea Free Trade Agreement was ratified by both governments in 2011 and went into effect in March 2012. Throughout 2012 the economy experienced sluggish growth because of market slowdowns in the United States, China, and the Eurozone. The incoming administration in 2013, following the December 2012 presidential election, is likely to face the challenges of balancing heavy reliance on exports with developing domestic-oriented sectors, such as services. The South Korean economy's long term challenges include a rapidly aging population, inflexible labor market, and heavy reliance on exports - which comprise half of GDP.

GDP (purchasing power parity):

$1.611 trillion (2012 est.)

country comparison to the world: 13

$1.579 trillion (2011 est.)

$1.524 trillion (2010 est.)

note: data are in 2012 US dollars

GDP (official exchange rate):

$1.151 trillion (2012 est.)

GDP - real growth rate:

2% (2012 est.)

country comparison to the world: 139

3.6% (2011 est.)

6.3% (2010 est.)

GDP - per capita (PPP):

$32,400 (2012 est.)

country comparison to the world: 43

$31,700 (2011 est.)

$30,800 (2010 est.)

note: data are in 2012 US dollars

GDP - composition by sector:

agriculture: 2.7%

industry: 39.8%

services: 57.5% (2012 est.)

Labor force:

25.5 million (2012 est.)

country comparison to the world: 25

Labor force - by occupation:

agriculture: 6.2%

industry: 23.8%

services: 70% (2012 est.)

Unemployment rate:

3.2% (2012 est.)

country comparison to the world: 26

3.4% (2011 est.)

Population below poverty line:

16.5% (2011 est.)

Household income or consumption by percentage share:

lowest 10%: 6.4%

highest 10%: 37.7% (2011)

Distribution of family income - Gini index:

41.9 (2011)

country comparison to the world: 51

35.8 (2000)

Investment (gross fixed):

25.2% of GDP (2012 est.)

country comparison to the world: 49

Budget:

revenues: $250.6 billion

expenditures: $243.9 billion (2012 est.)

Taxes and other revenues:

21.8% of GDP (2012 est.)

country comparison to the world: 146

Budget surplus (+) or deficit (-):

0.6% of GDP (2012 est.)

country comparison to the world: 33

Public debt:

33.7% of GDP (2012 est.)

country comparison to the world: 105

33.6% of GDP (2011 est.)

Inflation rate (consumer prices):

2.2% (2012 est.)

country comparison to the world: 41

4% (2011 est.)

Central bank discount rate:

1.5% (31 December 2011)

country comparison to the world: 132

1.25% (31 December 2009)

Commercial bank prime lending rate:

3.7% (31 December 2012 est.)

country comparison to the world: 145

5.77% (31 December 2011 est.)

Stock of narrow money:

$392 billion (31 December 2012 est.)

country comparison to the world: 14

$369.6 billion (31 December 2011 est.)

Stock of broad money:

$1.596 trillion (31 December 2012)

country comparison to the world: 12

$1.484 trillion (31 December 2011)

Stock of domestic credit:

$1.438 trillion (31 December 2012 est.)

country comparison to the world: 14

$1.356 trillion (31 December 2011 est.)

Market value of publicly traded shares:

$1.024 trillion (31 December 2012)

country comparison to the world: 15

$994.3 billion (31 December 2011)

$1.089 trillion (31 December 2010)

Agriculture - products:

rice, root crops, barley, vegetables, fruit; cattle, pigs, chickens, milk, eggs; fish

Industries:

electronics, telecommunications, automobile production,
chemicals, shipbuilding, steel

Industrial production growth rate:

1.7% (2012 est.)

country comparison to the world: 121

Current account balance:

$3.14 billion (2012 est.)

country comparison to the world: 34

$26.51 billion (2011 est.)

Exports:

$552.6 billion (2012 est.)

country comparison to the world: 8

$552.8 billion (2011 est.)

Exports - commodities:

semiconductors, wireless telecommunications equipment,
motor vehicles, computers, steel, ships, petrochemicals

Exports - partners:

China 24.4%, US 10.1%, Japan 7.1% (2011 est.)

Imports:

$514.2 billion (2012 est.)

country comparison to the world: 8

$521.6 billion (2011 est.)

Imports - commodities:

machinery, electronics and electronic equipment, oil, steel,
transport equipment, organic chemicals, plastics

Imports - partners:

China 16.5%, Japan 13%, US 8.5%, Saudi Arabia 7.1%, Australia 5% (2011 est.)

Reserves of foreign exchange and gold:

$326.9 billion (31 December 2012 est.)

country comparison to the world: 9

$306.4 billion (31 December 2011 est.)

Debt - external:

$413.4 billion (31 December 2012 est.)

country comparison to the world: 26

$449.6 billion (31 December 2011 est.)

Stock of direct foreign investment - at home:

$203.5 billion (31 December 2012 est.)

country comparison to the world: 22

$131.7 billion (31 December 2011 est.)

Stock of direct foreign investment - abroad:

$327.5 billion (31 December 2012)

country comparison to the world: 18

$190.4 billion (31 December 2011)

Exchange rates:

South Korean won (KRW) per US dollar -

1,126.8 (2012 est.)

1,108.29 (2011 est.)

1,156.1 (2010 est.)

1,276.93 (2009)

1,101.7 (2008)

Fiscal year:

calendar year

Chapter 6: Energy

Electricity - production:

    459.5 billion kWh (2011 est.)

    country comparison to the world: 12

Electricity - consumption:

    455.1 billion kWh (2011 est.)

    country comparison to the world: 10

Electricity - exports:

    0 kWh (2011)

    country comparison to the world: 215

Electricity - imports:

    0 kWh (2011)

    country comparison to the world: 206

Electricity - installed generating capacity:

    80.59 million kW (2009 est.)

    country comparison to the world: 14

Electricity - from fossil fuels:

    69.9% of total installed capacity (2009 est.)

    country comparison to the world: 106

Electricity - from nuclear fuels:

    22% of total installed capacity (2009 est.)

    country comparison to the world: 8

Electricity - from hydroelectric plants:

    2% of total installed capacity (2009 est.)

    country comparison to the world: 136

Electricity - from other renewable sources:

1.3% of total installed capacity (2009 est.)

country comparison to the world: 69

Crude oil - production:

19,990 bbl/day (2011 est.)

country comparison to the world: 73

Crude oil - exports:

0 bbl/day (2009 est.)

country comparison to the world: 138

Crude oil - imports:

2.59 million bbl/day (2012 est.)

country comparison to the world: 6

Crude oil - proved reserves:

NA bbl

Refined petroleum products - production:

2.83 million bbl/day (2012 est.)

country comparison to the world: 8

Refined petroleum products - consumption:

2.26 million bbl/day (2012 est.)

country comparison to the world: 11

Refined petroleum products - exports:

907,100 bbl/day (2009 est.)

country comparison to the world: 8

Refined petroleum products - imports:

753,900 bbl/day (2009 est.)

country comparison to the world: 9

Natural gas - production:

539.3 million cu m (2010 est.)

country comparison to the world: 72

Natural gas - consumption:

45.9 billion cu m (2011 est.)

country comparison to the world: 20

Natural gas - exports:

0 cu m (2011 est.)

country comparison to the world: 98

Natural gas - imports:

46.83 billion cu m (2011 est.)

country comparison to the world: 9

Natural gas - proved reserves:

5.748 billion cu m (1 January 2013 est.)

country comparison to the world: 87

Carbon dioxide emissions from consumption of energy:

579 million Mt (2010 est.)

country comparison to the world: 8

Chapter 7: Communications

Telephones - main lines in use:

29.468 million (2011)

country comparison to the world: 11

Telephones - mobile cellular:

52.507 million (2011)

country comparison to the world: 27

Telephone system:

general assessment: excellent domestic and international

services featuring rapid incorporation of new technologies

domestic: fixed-line and mobile-cellular services widely

available with a combined telephone subscribership of

roughly 170 per 100 persons; rapid assimilation of a full

range of telecommunications technologies leading to a

boom in e-commerce

international: country code - 82; numerous submarine

cables provide links throughout Asia, Australia, the

Middle East, Europe, and US; satellite earth stations - 66

Broadcast media:

multiple national TV networks with 2 of the 3 largest

networks publicly operated; the largest privately-owned

network, Seoul Broadcasting Service (SBS), has ties with

other commercial TV networks; cable and satellite TV

subscription services available; publicly-operated radio

broadcast networks and many privately-owned radio

broadcasting networks, each with multiple affiliates, and independent local stations (2010)

Internet country code:

.kr

Internet hosts:

315,697 (2012)

country comparison to the world: 62

Internet users:

39.4 million (2009)

country comparison to the world: 11

Chapter 8: Transportation

Airports:

> 114 (2012)

> country comparison to the world: 50

Airports - with paved runways:

> total: 71

> over 3,047 m: 4

> 2,438 to 3,047 m: 20

> 1,524 to 2,437 m: 12

> 914 to 1,523 m: 13

> under 914 m: 22 (2012)

Airports - with unpaved runways:

> total: 43

> 914 to 1,523 m: 2

> under 914 m: 41 (2012)

Heliports:

> 510 (2012)

Pipelines:

> gas 2,139 km; refined products 864 km (2010)

Railways:

> total: 3,381 km

> country comparison to the world: 51

> standard gauge: 3,381 km 1.435-m gauge (1,843 km electrified) (2008)

Roadways:

total: 103,029 km

country comparison to the world: 40

paved: 80,642 km (includes 3,367 km of expressways)

unpaved: 22,387 km (2008)

Waterways:

1,600 km (most navigable only by small craft) (2011)

country comparison to the world: 49

Merchant marine:

total: 786

country comparison to the world: 14

by type: bulk carrier 191, cargo 235, carrier 8, chemical tanker 130, container 72, liquefied gas 44, passenger 5, passenger/cargo 15, petroleum tanker 55, refrigerated cargo 15, roll on/roll off 10, vehicle carrier 6

foreign-owned: 31 (China 6, France 2, Japan 14, Taiwan 1, US 8)

registered in other countries: 457 (Bahamas 1, Cambodia 10, Ghana 1, Honduras 6, Hong Kong 3, Indonesia 2, Kiribati 1, Liberia 2, Malta 2, Marshall Islands 41, North Korea 1, Panama 373, Philippines 1, Russia 1, Singapore 3, Tuvalu 1, unknown 8) (2010)

Ports and terminals:

Incheon (Inch'on), Pohang (P'ohang), Busan (Pusan), Ulsan, Yeosu (Yosu)

Chapter 9: Military

Military branches:

> Republic of Korea Army, Navy (includes Marine Corps), Air Force (2011)

Military service age and obligation:

> 20-30 years of age for compulsory military service, with middle school education required; conscript service obligation - 21 months (Army, Marines), 23 months (Navy), 24 months (Air Force); 18-26 years of age for voluntary military service; women, in service since 1950, admitted to 7 service branches, including infantry, but excluded from artillery, armor, anti-air, and chaplaincy corps; HIV-positive individuals are exempt from military service (2010)

Manpower available for military service:

> males age 16-49: 13,185,794
>
> females age 16-49: 12,423,496 (2010 est.)

Manpower fit for military service:

> males age 16-49: 10,864,566
>
> females age 16-49: 10,168,709 (2010 est.)

Manpower reaching militarily significant age annually:

> male: 365,760
>
> female: 321,225 (2010 est.)

Military expenditures:

> 2.7% of GDP (2006)

Chapter 10: Transnational Issues

Disputes - international:

Military Demarcation Line within the 4-km-wide Demilitarized Zone has separated North from South Korea since 1953; periodic incidents with North Korea in the Yellow Sea over the Northern Limit Line, which South Korea claims as a maritime boundary; South Korea and Japan claim Liancourt Rocks (Tok-do/Take-shima), occupied by South Korea since 1954

Map of South Korea

Other Key Facts™ Titles

Key Facts on Iraq

Key Facts on Indonesia

All Key Facts™ Titles are Available at

www.Amazon.com

THE INTERNATIONALIST®

2013

www.internationalist.com